1

UNLEASHING YOUR INNER WARRIOR GODDESS

KIM BOWIE

Editor: Write Way Editorial Services

Book Cover and Formatting: Remember To ThinkPink Publications© DALLAS, TEXAS.

This book is Dedicated to the old Kim. All the tears you cried, the disappointments, and heartbreaks you experienced were for this moment right here, right now.

You fought a good fight, but I could not properly reign in my universe as THIS KIM without chopping off your head.

You've conquered a lot of territory in your reign and there are still battles ahead. You will have the victory. Kim, I love you more and more every day. As you move forward, remember that nothing is real, and anything is possible.

FOREWORD

Thankfully, Kim Bowie has written a how to guide to instruct women on how to awaken the warrior goddess within. Though it may be casually cataloged as a self-help book it is more of a self-empowering, self-engaging, self-awakening book. "Unleashing Your Inner Warrior Goddess" is a step-by-step instructional manual for women that leads the reader on her own journey of awakening. Instead of using popular psycho-babble, the author plainly details an easily understandable 7-step process that takes the reader from a point of complacency to full awareness and participation in creating her own reality. Using her own personal experience as an example, Bowie demonstrates the practical application of the steps in her own life. Her transparency, passion, and conversational writing style left me feeling as if I had a session with a skillful and intuitive life coach or therapist. I was inspired to conquer the demons within to recognize and unleash the power I was created with. Bowie guides you through the process to find your own answers and reasons for awakening your warrior goddess.

This freshman offering by Kim Bowie is well-written and organized in such a way you can read it in one sitting. However, the content will follow you and spur you into action. "Unleashing Your Warrior Goddess" should be required reading by all women seeking greater awareness. Written by a powerful woman who is willing to share her experiential knowledge, this book encourages other women to discover their own source of power—their own warrior goddess.

- by R. J. Trout

INTRODUCTION

I have always loved stories of women who defied the odds and marched to the beat of their own drum. My favorite Bible story is the story of Judith (found in the Apocrypha). Here, we have this powerful woman who had to cease mourning her husband's untimely death to go save her nation. The enemy had surrounded Israel's camp and cut off their water supply. Israel's enemy was ready to celebrate their victory and Israel's leaders put up no fight. They told the people, "We are going to need to start consuming less water and if God doesn't save us over the next 5 days, prepare yourselves for surrender to the Assyrian army."

Judith hears of her people's act of desperation and said, "Not today, Israel!" She sent for the elders and once they arrived, she rebuked them for their lack of trust in God, then she notified them of her plan to gain victory for Israel. She was discreet and gave very little details.

Prior to the execution of her plan, Judith spent all her time in the "upper room" building up her strength and confidence for the victory at hand. Once she had received her power, she and her maid begin preparing for their journey. They chose and blessed specific foods. Judith took off her widow's attire and put on that "Yes, I'm here dress," then applied her red lips. She grabbed her maid and made their way to the Assyrian camp.

Upon their arrival, the men were captivated by her beauty. The Assyrian men said, "If these are the type of women that Israel produces, we must kill every man in that camp." They hung onto every word she told them. The Assyrian men willingly delivered her to their leader, Holofernes. When Judith met with Holofernes, he was astounded by her appearance and assured her she would be safe in the Assyrian camp. He then inquired about her arrival, and Judith convinced him that Israel was being punished for a particular sin, that the Assyrians would gain victory over the

Israelites, and that she was trying to find a safe place before everything hit the fan.

Within 4 days of Judith's arrival, Holofernes hosted a feast in his tent and invited Judith to dine with him. She did not eat the food he presented to her; instead, she was nourished only by the food that she had blessed before the start of her journey. Holofernes became extremely excited by Judith's presence and continued to drink excessive amounts of wine until he was drunk. Once the banquet was over, everyone left his tent except for Judith. She knew, "This is my moment to gain victory for my people!" As he laid passed out on his bed, Judith had her maid watch the door. She approached his bed, grabbed hold of his hair and called on her God. With two strikes of his sword, she held the head of her enemy in her hands.

This story played a pivotal part in me realizing who I am as a woman, warrior, and a goddess. Judith gave me a greater understanding of the tools that I had access to in this realm.

I watched as Judith refused to open the door to defeat when it knocked, then stepped into her divine power like a pair of pants. She used her sexuality and glamour to win victory for her nation. She was an excellent example of going within for answers needed. I watched her utilize specific foods for her journey, all while having very little outward communication during her preparation. We live in a society where we know how to beautify our outward shell, but the development of our powers stop there. We lack the ability to do internal work while living whole lives with no idea who we are and what we are truly capable of.

I remember hearing the story of a woman whose child was stuck under the wheel of a car, and the mother lifted the car to save her child. I have met individuals who refuse to live in poverty another generation; they have created generational wealth in some mind-blowing ways. There are people who have cured themselves of diseases that the medical world said were incurable. I'm watching others tap into their power daily while I sit back trying to figure out how I can pierce through the veil to access my power. I know it's more to me but how do I get to it? I know, and can explain to you, that there is an infinite, powerful force dwelling in each and every single part of me that I cannot be separated from. But where is this part of me really located? How do I wake it up for the big stuff in my life? I know if I find it, it would be unstoppable. This force is capable of absolutely anything that I could imagine. This is the part of my being where the miraculous and extraordinary part of me dwells. It continually tugs at me. It whispers to me throughout the day and wrestles with me in my sleep. It is constantly attempting to show me what I am truly capable of. This is not the most dominant part of my personality; however, it can be.

Each one of us is carrying unique gifts within. They came to you for you to give them life. They are waiting anxiously to come alive and be free. The words written in this book are about a mental accumulation, an internal expansion, and an emotional evolution. This new shift will cost you, you. It can and should be applied to every part of your life.

When we look back at history, there are several powerful women who did extraordinary, unfathomable things. Some of my personal favorites: Madam CJ Walker, Queen Nzinga, Marian Anderson, just to name a few. These women with all their many different stories tapped into their power. They were pioneers that paved new ground. They woke up their inner warrior goddess. Join me on the journey of the recalibration of my mind as I share the lessons I learned to unleash my warrior goddess.

CHAPTER ONE

WHAT IS A WARRIOR GODDESS?

Before I give you the definition, allow me to remind you who you are as a woman. You are a medium. You are the vehicle used to transmit between two realms.

You can bring life from the spiritual realm into this physical realm that we call earth. Sit with that for a moment. It is possible that you've never looked at it from this perspective.

Whether or not you have used your body in that manner, you were innately created with the gift of doing so.

Allow me to put yet another spin on this. If you can tap into the spiritual realm to bring forth life in the physical realm, you can do this with anything.

You can tap into the spiritual realm to give birth to your wealth, your health, and anything you can imagine. The only limitation you have is your mind, and you control that.

Firstly, a warrior goddess is a warrior who knows how to access her divine power as she wages war for everything that is rightfully hers. She is a nurturer, a protector, a healer, and a sexual being.

Once she begins to tap into these different parts of her nature, she simultaneously wakes up different parts of her power.

The warrior goddess must become the first partaker of these characteristics. She must learn to nurture herself first, then she will automatically begin to nurture her environment. She must learn to properly go to war for herself, in that she will learn to become a warrior for her surroundings. Once she heals herself she has now tapped into her healing energy. See how this works? You must apply your oxygen mask first.

As we start this journey, there are some other tools and weapons we will need to develop.

CHAPTER TWO

WEAPON #1: SELF-CONFIDENCE

*"Confidence is not 'they will like me.'
Confidence is 'I'll be fine if they don't.'"*

—Christina Grimmie

Self-confidence: an awareness of your power.

We have been raised in an atmosphere that teaches us to look outside of ourselves for our power. As you embark on this pilgrimage, your confidence will be extremely important in every aspect of who you are. How you view yourself will be the foundation that you stand on. Self-confidence is simply learning to love yourself and appreciate who you are and what you bring to the table. For most of us, life has taught us that we're not good enough and we don't matter.

Permit me to remind you that you are a kickass woman! There is absolutely nothing you can't do!

I started working on my confidence in my 20s, but was well into my 30s before I realized the confidence I thought I had was coming from the outside versus from within.

When something on the outside of you defines how you feel internally, it is circumstantial. We cannot build a solid foundation from outside resources when it comes to our confidence. Trust me, this does you no favors. Just like a dog can smell fear, humans can sense your lack of confidence and they will play on your weaknesses.

I could no longer spend days worrying about the past or daydreaming about the future. When I became present and conscious at that moment, it gave me the ability to respond in situations from a place of power.

I may have been a thirty-plus-year-old woman, but inside I was still that little ten-year-old girl. She was waving her hands saying, "Hey, I'm over here. Pick me! See me." For me to move on and

build my confidence I had to give her—
my inner child—what she had been
lacking all of these years. She needed
love and support and to know that she
mattered.

Most importantly she needed to know
that she was safe. I couldn't expect, nor
was it anyone else's job, to heal her. I
had to learn what it meant to see myself
and to choose myself first. I had to learn
to trust what I had been given and to
truly honor my feelings. I had to embrace
every ounce of uniqueness that flowed
through my veins, then dominate those
members of my physical being that
didn't want to line up with my new
thought process.

It is vital that you understand and analyze
where your leaks are in terms of your
self-confidence. Here are some questions
that you can use to evaluate the position
of your confidence. They may take you
some time to answer, and that's okay
because I want you to take the time to
evaluate yourself when answering them.
Who are you? What areas in your life

have you given your power away? What have you told yourself is required of you to be accepted by other people?

What does confidence look like?

When no one's opinion outside of yours matters. I'm not telling you to throw out wise counsel, but no one's voice should weigh heavier than what you are feeling in your spirit. You have the final say in the moves you make.

The more you work to develop confidence in your own voice, the more you will see yourself standing in your power. This growth comes in layers like an onion. There will always be another level to reach.

I invite you to develop and to cultivate the confidence in yourself. This is the beginning of you walking and living in your power. No one can give this to you, you must go and get it for yourself.

Here are a few exercises you can do to grow your confidence.

Exercises to Build Confidence

- Make a list of your strengths & weaknesses.
- Chose a positive thought about yourself to meditate on all day.
- Kill every negative thought that comes to your mind.
- Practice being more assertive.
- Do something special for yourself.
- Take more bubble baths.
- Put more effort in how you present yourself to the world.
- Have no makeup days.
- Cut your hair.
- Add more fruit & veggies to your diet.
- Exercise.
- Start journaling.
- Meditate.
- Visualize yourself as you want to be and then be it.
- Create daily affirmations.
- Do something that scares you.
- Help someone.
- Practice saying no.

CHAPTER THREE
Weapon #2: NEGOTIATING

"Sell or be sold."—Greg Cardone

Negotiate: when two or more parties come together to agree on the terms of their future dealings.

Once I became fully present and engaged in my own life, I learned that I was constantly sitting at a negotiation table for many different situations. Due to my lack of confidence, I realized that I either showed up to the table late or sometimes not at all. When I did show up, I only demanded the bare minimum from the other party. This is no way to live.

There was this one time I fell deeply in love with this man. He was everything! I declared This Man was going to be my husband. I was so smitten by his majestic, country traits that I disregarded the words he spoke at our negotiation table. I was actually at the altar wishing he would hurry up and get there. Early in our relationship he got custody of his three young children. Because I was focused on making this man my husband at any cost, I easily confused his need for help with the children with him being deeply in love with me. I would work at night then go and keep his kids all day while he went to work. I was a good step-mommy, but still ignoring the words he spoke when we were at the negotiation table. After a few months, the children returned to their mother and he returned to the mindset he informed me of in the beginning.

I worked a very demanding job that took up a lot of my time. I didn't meet the company's "criteria" for a full-time employee, even though I was giving this job full-time hours out of my life, I was ineligible for benefits.

One day, I showed up at the negotiation table. I demanded more from my relationship and although it ended, my eyes were open to the lie I was living and the fact that I deserved more than what I was receiving. I went to my job and demanded benefits in my current employment status and I got them.

When I began to show up for me, that's when I began to see what I wanted show up in my life. Everything is for sale. Negotiations are taking place in every single aspect of your life. Someone is always out to capitalize on you in some manner and you must show up to the table to get what you want out of life.

We walk around with little or no confidence and we lose our voice. When someone offers us the crumbs off their table, we take them. We have yet to discover that we have our own personal seat just for us at the table.

No one or nothing can pull you out of ignorance. You must do the work to dig yourself out of that ditch. Break up your own fallow ground.

We leave our lives in the hands of other people, while doing very little to steer it in the direction we want it to go. We must be willing to walk away from anything that does not serve us and is not willing to adjust to our needs.

When we show up to the negotiating table we conquer our fear. Ultimately, fear is the root of our issue. We are scared to speak up because we fear to lose what we have.

We're immersed in thoughts that say, "I'm not worthy of it, so however you give it to me, I'll take it."

That, my sister, is no longer your truth. You will stand in your GODFIDENCE (Godly confidence) and demand what is yours. Then be willing to walk away if your needs are not met. This starts with you; demand of yourself to start showing up to the negotiation table for your own life.

You will no longer live in a world where other people are making decisions about you and your life without your presence or permission.

It is your birthright to CHOOSE where you want to live and how you want your

life to look. YOU ALWAYS HAVE A
CHOICE! The climb to the top will be
challenging, as there are some muscles
that you've never used. However, start
climbing—that's how the muscles
develop. I am a firm believer that if you
take one step, GOD takes two.

Here are ways to show up to the
negotiation table for yourself:

- Practice saying no.
- Set boundaries and honor them.
- Pay attention to how you feel in
  different situations.
- Be willing to walk away.
- Speak up.
- Listen to your intuition.
- Pay attention to the words people
  speak.

CHAPTER FOUR

Weapon #3: EMBRACING YOUR PAIN

"Man is a star bounded to a body until the end. He is freed through his strife. Only by struggle and toil will the star within you bloom with new life."

—*the Emerald Tablet*

We try to avoid pain at all costs. We even try to shield our loved ones from it, but the way this life is set up, it can't be avoided by you, me, or anyone else.

We have inadequately handled our pain. We have tried sweeping it under the rug as if it didn't exist. We buried it deeply, or so we thought.

Let me let you in on a secret: our pain will continue to show up in our lives until we deal with it. We will have the same situation repeat itself over and over until we decide to stand toe to toe with it.

27

We even pass it down to our children when we decide not to deal with it.

Start looking at your pain differently. Pain is here to serve you. It's here to help you grow. When you conquer your pain, it becomes the stool you stand on to go to your next level.

For the pain to serve you, you must shift your perception about it. Face it. Stand in it. It's in that moment that true healing and evolution can take place in your life. This may be an uncomfortable process, but you must allow yourself to go through it, feel your pain, and ask, "What are you here to teach me?"

What do you feel like doing? Do you want to kick the wall? Kick it. Do you feel like crying? Cry. Do you want to beat somebody up? Okay, I don't recommend that, but maybe go to the gym and release all that anger on a boxing bag. When we decide not to face our fears and pain they become magnets drawing themselves to us over and over again, creating blockages, which create dis-ease in our bodies.

One day I was watching the show "Being Mary Jane." On this episode Mary Jane did a story about a young lady who died and her body sat on the couch decomposing for months before anyone realized she was dead. This particular episode was extremely sorrowful for me. It affected me for weeks. As I watched this show, the energy of loneliness came and sat on my lap. I had been stewing in this thought for years: I will die alone and no one would immediately miss my presence from this planet. My secret thoughts were now being played across my 50-inch television. Defeat is disrespectful. This was my greatest fear. Being alone was painful for me even to think about. I had to make a decision, will I go and put my red lips on, step into my power, and contend with my greatest antagonist? Or do I allow fear to continue to grip me and squeeze every bit of life out of me until that very scenario becomes my truth? I was tired of that fear continually knocking at my door. I was tired of making bad decisions trying to avoid it and it still making its way to my lap.

At some point, you will have to do the work. Sit in it, allow the pain to teach you the lesson it was sent here to teach. There will be some rough days, but continue moving forward. Nothing stays the same. It will get easier. Then one day it won't even bother you anymore.

When I faced my greatest fear, I found that greater part of me. When I conquered that mountain, I found my wealth. I had to contend with my greatest enemy to get access to it.

Take some time and meditate on the things you been through in this life. Ask those experiences, "What did you come to teach me?"

CHAPTER FIVE

Weapon #4: YOUR POWER

"To be powerful means you have the ability to say no."

—Balah the Experience

Who are the powerful individuals in your life? Your boss? Your loan officer? What makes them powerful? Simply put, they are powerful because they can tell you no.

Each and everyone one of us are very powerful beings. We have the power to produce an effect. Most of us do not utilize our power.

I took my niece to the Florida Keys for her graduation. We flew into Miami and our plan was to take the Greyhound down to the Keys. We got to the bus station and no buses were leaving until 6 a.m. the next morning, and at this time it was only 7 p.m. So, we go to catch a cab back to the airport and two cab drivers started fighting over who was going to serve us. One cab driver took our bags and put them in his cab when the other driver yelled out, "He's going to rob you. Don't get in his cab!"

At this point, I was having a full-blown freak-out! I snapped out of my panic when I heard my eighteen-year-old niece in all her glorious power yell, "GIVE US OUR STUFF!"

Suddenly both cab drivers stopped fighting and handed us our belongings. We called another cab and headed back to the airport peacefully.

I like to use this as a prime example of the internal war inside each of us and what it looks like to stand in your power or to choose not to.

I made the decision to give in to my lower self, and my fear won. I did not take control of my mind, which produced panic and added to the chaos.

Quite honestly, this incident could have had an unfavorable end. My niece, on the other hand, was the perfect example of making a firm decision and executing actions based on that decision, because she took control of her mind and emotions. She said no and demanded actions with it. Because of this, we made it safely to the Florida Keys and we enjoyed a week of beautiful sunshine on the beach.

Watching my niece in action put a beaming light on my weakness and prompted me to deal with the parts of me that were timid and afraid.

To be powerful means that you can say no, and you MUST use that ability. You must learn to say no to yourself and to others. When we admire and respect discipline in others, we're watching power in action.

That person who is disciplined with their diet or workout regimen had the power to say no to themselves when they wanted that piece of cake or didn't want to go to the gym.

Power is saying no to the dynamics of a relationship no longer work for you—

whether it's your boss, spouse, or your banker. No! Power is the ability to say "NO." You will not give me less than what I deserve. I realized I am the bottom line for my life, the conduit makes this happen…knowing the power of no and how it can be moved in any direction I want it to go, that it was all up to me.

We must take responsibility for the energy introduced into our presence and guide it in the direction in which it needs to leave. Sometimes it needs to be guided out the front door.

I had to awaken this power, MY power. If I didn't, I would continue to be a doormat to my emotions and fear. I welcome you to do the same for yourself.

CHAPTER SIX

Weapon #5: OPPOSITION

*"You will never advance if you keep
going back to your place of comfort."*

— Chelsea Bowie

Let me let you in on a secret. I don't care
what you're doing, YOU WILL FACE
OPPOSITION. Whether you decide to
have a baby, get married, start a business,
or just simply wake up. The opposition
will be knocking at your door. This
chapter of the book is to sound the alarm
so that when challenges show up, they
won't catch you off guard.

This is simple yet profound. Something
in us wants to believe that everything
will be perfect all the time; it will, just
not in this realm.

Creation can only take place in a
balanced atmosphere. So, the dark and
light, the Yin and the Yang must be
present with everything that is created.

Whatever the opposition is, it's here to serve you. Your job is to work through it. When we push through and challenge the comfortable and frightened parts of ourselves we wake up more of our divine power.

I remember watching "The Oprah Winfrey Show." She had a young lady of middle eastern decent on whose husband had set her on fire. She was a beautiful woman before the fire. She now sat on the show with melted facial features and her skin from her face to her neck and the features underneath were without definition.

She told Oprah, "I only give myself 5 minutes at a time to cry." She didn't deny herself the tears, but she didn't soak in them. When the 5 minutes are up, she gets up, stands in her power, and moves forward.

Acknowledge the opposition.

Create a ritual to align you with your higher power.

This can be through prayer, mirror talk, journaling, boxing the air, or some other form of stimulation that allows you to align your mental, physical, and spiritual being. Then grab your power and move forward.

You may have to do this exercise every twenty minutes in the beginning but do it and keep doing it. It will help you conquer and move pass this opposition.

CHAPTER SEVEN

Weapon #6: BE INTENTIONAL

"Live less out of habit and more out of intent."—unknown

Allow me to create a visual about who you are. You are a spiritual being. Now let's take and put you on a spectrum. In your mind's eye create a horizontal line with two points at either end. When you entered the earth realm you came with everything in you to live wherever you want to live on that spectrum. So, if you decide to live on the lower end of the spectrum, just do the norm. Continue to entertain lower vibrational thought forms. These thoughts consist of depression, poverty, illness, and any type of lack. This will keep you functioning at the bottom of your spectrum. Or you can entertain the thoughts of progression, blissfulness, health, wealth, and any type of abundance. Thinking about these things will help push you to the other end of your spectrum.

With this in mind, let us discuss intentions and affirmations. These are some tools that will assist with the movement of you on your spectrum. Now let us define Intentions and affirmations. **Intention** (Webster): what one intends to do, to stretch out or lay out the future plans. **Affirmation**: to declare the truth or existence of something. So, when you use these tools, imagine yourself laying out, or stretching into these words you speak. To use these tools, you must make a decision about who you are and who you want to be, then begin to speak and call that version of you forth. Keep speaking it until you feel it with everything in you. You can choose to be anything you desire to be. I would advise you to dream big. Don't limit yourself; this act is waking up the God part of you. Any thought that comes to you is proof that it's in your energetic field and you have the ability to call it forth. This is the importance of having strong confidence. Good, strong, balanced confidence in yourself produces confidence in the words you speak. A person that is confident in the words they speak understands the creative force in their words. This understanding brings about less idle chatter because this person knows every day is a judgment day and they will give an account for the words they speak, good or bad. So they choose their words wisely.

Confidence in the words you speak will also bring you to a place of rest, your Sabbath. When you have surety about the words you speak, you enter into a place of peace. You're not in mental chaos behind the change that needs to come about. You go make love to your spouse, take a nap, or even count the hairs on your leg. In your mind, it is finished. When we enter into God's nature, the miraculous becomes our norm.

This is one of the most powerful things you can do. This is really an act of dominance. It's your birthright. The second chapter of Hebrews reminds us to hold on to this truth: that God has given us complete charge over everything. Everything! You can begin to take charge over everything by the words you speak.

Your words are spirit and they will not return to you void. What are you creating with your words?

You can start by beginning to set intentions over the water you are about to drink, the food you are about to eat, the day you are going to have. You're tapping into your GOD-given power.

When you meet someone new, set the intention for that relationship. By doing so, you are being conscious at that moment and tapping into the power of life and death that dwells in your tongue. This is a powerful tool to use. You are not utilizing your gifts you came to earth with when you don't take dominion over your life. You no longer have to live a life where you allow just anything to happen to you without your permission.

I invite you to begin to set intentions over everything you do and encounter. Command the day you are about to embark on.

CHAPTER EIGHT

Weapon #7: THE POWER OF KNOWING

"When you know yourself, you are empowered. When you accept yourself, you are invincible."- Tina Lifford

Everything I have written about are tools to help you tap into the bliss of awareness of self. Who are you?

I've heard this question asked for years. Most people can't answer it.

It has often been defined by what a person does or their relations with others. To answer the question of who you are has nothing to do with anything outside of you, but everything within you.

One day I was getting dressed to go out on the town with my cousin. I had Farrakhan playing in the background. As I'm looking in the mirror making sure my makeup was on point, my cousin enters the room and stares at me for a second and then asks, "What type of human are you?" (That's the clean version.) We laughed, headed out, and enjoyed our evening.

It took me a long time to be okay with the answer to that question. I'm different. I'm eccentric, awkward, and an introvert sometimes. I am also amongst the greatest who have ever walked this earth. I am a pioneer. I go ahead and clear the path for those to follow. So my actions will never look like others. I show you what's possible. I love all things spiritual, I hug trees, I talk to my ancestors, I'm writing this book with crystals in my bra.

On this journey, self-awareness is a must. If I'm an introvert and trying to live a life of an extrovert, I'm in the wrong lane and I cannot be my divine self in the wrong lane. We run from our uniqueness and that's where our power lies. I am the only me.

As you learn to use your weapons found in this book, the 7th weapon of knowing is developed on its own. It is a freebie! You just have to pay attention to you.

This knowledge was developed as I worked on the other parts of me. I now know who I am.

I am convinced that I am a child of GOD! I am a woman! I am a healer, warrior, a teacher. I bring value everywhere I go. These characteristics make me a powerful being and I understand there is nothing I cannot do. I have the universe sitting on top of my shoulders. Because I know this, no one can take it from me and I will use every single tool I have access to. My actions show it. I walk in it and I get stronger every day.

I invite you to write a "who you are" statement. Stand in the mirror and speak it. Yell it until it becomes a part of your DNA, flowing through every part of your being.

CONCLUSION

On this journey it is easier to focus our attention on the cares of this world versus doing the work. You continue staying in situations where you know "this ain't it." We go to jobs that we hate, because this is how you pay rent. That's why you were created to pay rent, right? NO! You are here to become your greatest you. Every new day that you wake up is another chance for you to conquer more land, move your life forward. This book consists of the 7 tools I used to move my life forward and to tap into my power. Sometimes the simplest things challenge us the most. We are developing new habits and it's easier to do what we've been doing. The fact that you're reading this book is evident that I pushed passed my comfort zone. I treaded some new ground and chopped the head of some old, limiting thought patterns. You are not reading this book by accident. I pray wherever you are in life, that by the end of this book, you receive more clarity for your pilgrimage. I pray that you tap into the divine feminine warrior you are and wake up all the powerful gifts that you came to the earth with. It is time to wake up the warrior within.

Kimberley Bowie

ACKNOWLEDGMENTS

I would like to acknowledge my spiritual army. Thank you. Thank you for your shoulders that I stand on that allow me to see beyond the horizon.

To my mother, I wondered why we showed up this way together in this season of our lives. I soon realized you have ingredients that I need for the recipes I'm cooking. And I in return have some ingredients for yours. God has granted us a do-over. This time we get to do it with the wisdom we didn't have twenty years ago. Cycles are being broken and we are healing our DNA— past, present, and future.

To the great wise one, thank you. You saw me when I thought no one was looking. You are an astute observer and you have invested in me wisely.

To Ms. Blue and Brother Balah & the "Remix Family." Thank you for showing me how to wake her up more and more every day. You helped me make sense of all this information in my head. You showed me my tools in my toolbox and how to use them. There are times I don't even recognize the woman I am, and for that, I will be forever grateful.

To all the women that will wake up their warrior from reading this book. I say ASÉ.

Kim Bowie is a native of Ohio but felt drawn to plant her roots in Texas. She received her degree in nursing from Columbus State and she is a Holistic Practitioner and a spiritual Life Coach.

Kim is the founder of Lethal Lady Enterprises where she lives in her passion of empowering women in every area of their lives.

43618481R00031

Made in the USA
Middletown, DE
26 April 2019